Molly the Menorah

Written by C.E. Grossman
Illustrated by Anna Perevalova

Molly the Menorah

Story © 2023 C.E. Grossman Illustrations © 2023 Anna Perevalova

All rights reserved.

No part of this publication may be reproduced, stored in a retrieval system, or transmitted in any form or by any means, electronic, mechanical, photocopying, recording, or otherwise, without the written permission of the publisher except for the use of brief quotations in a book review.

Illustrated by Anna Perevalova

Written by C.E. Grossman

First Edition: 2023

To
SOPHIE + SKYLAR

Once upon a time, in a far away town,
lived a menorah named Molly, who was red, gold and brown.
With candles shining bright, she brought warmth and cheer,
every night of Hanukkah, spreading joy far and near.

On night one, Molly spoke with delight,
"Did you know that Hanukkah starts tonight?
For eight special nights, we kindle candles with care,
to celebrate the miracle that happened over there."

As the second night arrived, Molly shared her tale,
"Long ago, brave Maccabees did prevail.
They fought for freedom, oh so bold,
and in the Holy Temple, a miracle did unfold."

On the third night Molly's glow filled the room,
"Oil was running low, starting to cause gloom.
But a small jug was found, just enough for a day,
yet it burned for eight nights, lighting the way."

The fourth night came and Molly continued her rhyme,
"Gather 'round the menorah, it's storytime.
We play a game with a spinning dreidel,
and eat matzo ball soup, straight from the ladle."

The fifth night arrived, Molly smiled with pride,
"The menorah's light, it cannot hide.
We place it by the window, for all to see,
a symbol of hope, for everyone to be free."

On the sixth night, Molly's flames danced with grace,
"Latkes we fry, a delicious embrace."

The seventh night approached, Molly's light grew bright,
"Families come together on this special night.

"We exchange gifts, spreading love and cheer, the tradition of Hanukkah grows year after year."

On the eighth and final night, Molly's light was still bright.
"This is not over, the celebration forever takes flight!

There she was, glowing fully completely.
Hanukkah now understood, as her light grew deeply.
With each glowing candle she glimmered with glee.
A symbol of harmony, for all to see.

Manufactured by Amazon.ca
Bolton, ON